SUSQUEHANNA

Cover images:
"chair" and "books" by c.smith
2012

Cover and Interior Design by Cassandra Smith

Typefaces: Adobe Caslon Pro and Cochin LT STD

Offset Printed on
Glatfelter 55# Natures Book Natural (30% PCW)
FSC Certified Archival Quality Acid Free Recycled Paper

Cataloguing-in-Publication Data is available from the Library of Congress.

Published by Omnidawn Publishing, Richmond, California
www.omnidawn.com   (510) 237-5472   (800) 792-4957
10 9 8 7 6 5 4 3 2 1
ISBN: 978-1-890650-84-1

susquehanna

G.C. Waldrep

omnidawn publishing
richmond, california
2013

1.

foglight in the electric
laurel   fanlight penetralia
as a fox is
a few thousand years
made liquid   scarlet

trousseau or   sphagnum
this human industry
compressed into earth-
rudder's   second emptiness

braids a fist, lengthwise

bruised toadflax
on the scull-cap's path or
plaint   —but rivers

the wheedling ash-breath

cleft / bloodroot
submarine in equinoctial
escheat   the hunter's
thriveling   scry-maple

2.

spay the yews' death-
thatch, core-beaded

spay the hawthorn's
grey aura   o come o

Act   o fractional
deleterious   revealed

premonstratensian

sucks the smaller organs
(clear of the body)

3.

under the mullein's
brads' rude chapbook

flydreaming gash &

what spirits farm this
intrusion / botanizing

surveyor's transit

4.

Warum in the blacklick
blood-glutened   clean
burin laid up against
all vigor's emerald blade

pared as silhouette
from amazement's cross-
grained inflorescence
dead-nettle eeling
into pigweed, chicory

not hooks nor earth-
works' heavy belaying
enharmonic / the animal
finish   broadcasting

the heron's veery spilth

5.

low chant, the slurry dam's
mangle in spawnlight
doweled into the actual
percussion   (stone
but not in any   usual way)

6.

or weight—the loosestrife's
profligate currency, is
thaumatrope (mauve + white)

is / (is not)   "local"

7.

saltation   ply-hour

smooth encaustic drift
poplar-musk, all voice &
spunky undercarriage

annealed, the young
approach the mask(s)
with no less reverence

gutters the watch-
tower's florid carom

rucked muslin against
the river's red thigh

8.

hythe-bright chapel

the carter's plastron &
drugged carapace

lustrous epistrophe

made nervous in
the factories' steepled
primelight

quickening flag-brush

or   plash-ruptured

9.

the mirror's acid breath
imbricates, muscle-scripted

cartouche   collodion

the tongue extends,
grey-battured implement

left squatting in pelf

made, then   o splendor
of the left hand's rebarbative
camera-island, its gold

catenary, its *cataract-lymph*

10.

subsumed refrangency
the eye-bridge   *encloses,*

louder than beckon or
web-arsenal, blue tarmac

in briefer mount, porcelain
diptych of volition's
nubile armaments, *will*

climb trees for the blood—

or   splaycasting choir

11.

this pattern cinders music

12.

embanked charterhouse
of storm on potter's
inner bank & sandy weir

straddling the mute
underpass   periphrastic
jeweled with hermitage

perfumed indulgencies
of the boneyard, you hear

but do not see
the owl's stiff fascination

13.

the way the beehive kilns
whisper *dear friends*
—*Let's not do that again*

swart corm, ruddled
in dew season, procumbent
erect & thus do fenestrate

all names are younger here

14.

coitus of the soil's
actinic deafchant, thinned
to milk-mask

pathetically small,
the mare-mange lights it

I greet you, &   —I
greet you
(—cradling water-monk)

15.

downriver   the mind's
sward or swathe
aureoled & astered

gunning against its axis

is not impact-lucid
if / (not   : neotenous)

pandect thrush of
bituminous cathexis

caryatid   colophon
vs. thyme's dorsal brace

16.

solve for   [Dresden,
Belfast] —nightlash, o

breeding ordinary thing

ground to stubble's
cross-chunter & dubbed

into pure (haulm)-life

17.

not the river's voice
for all your
standing vertebrae

this oak passes

through bees'
enameling dream
or study-map

distal anther chapel

vigia or   neolithic

18.

false-flaring eight-point
physicality   vaporing

into the spoor-substrate

19.

the ear's intaglio spathe
star-necked pyrography
enfolds, some egg section
& rhythmic in their scale

puncheon of hypnotic

mass extinctions, a scent

(dead-weighting
the cartridge-spine's
epidermal bore

nothing you see here
is ghost   but   Man
in his hedge-vessel

& leather catheter
polishes a slow gun)

20.

taste its bandage
of drenched tunelight

some frizzled pylon or
(mixed) wound-totem

rib-bracken   hive-
warder, -sentry, -verger

we shall not mast
this sudden ark & flay

21.

marled & limpsy, robber-
flow juddering indigo
against the harebells'
passacaglia   —eclectic

boon-harrier at dusk

brushing back the voice's
preposterous nail,

its blood-scented foil

reprise of hellebore
thrumming   covert / or
noctilucent, some think

death goes unreported

22.

basswood enshrapneling
the visitors' pool, not less
travel for the heel's

prehensile alluvion

shawmed in may-castor
the span's harvest vector
infiltrates &, open-
throated, the ripe jack's acid

broadcasts (genuflects)

little depth-shifts in
the old-growth occupation

23.

trigonal   fawn-in-glide

beech-cyst & Unhand
this heavy denizen   —I
solder my own life
to the instrument's flank

tawny   throat's
slow ratchet flung

into the half-pipe glade

my sweet   nude of
hysterical geophagy
tumbling tetherward

under the gill-chimneys

24.

under the pink glove

seasonal longhouse
cascade of   shelter-
fleck or ragged cog
in the skeining gloam

under the roe-lesion
under the buck

under the sign
of the falling bear

what cannot farrow-I

the sediment husk
vetched in cleave-hand

to dream of—
(quickening spline)
that thaw   again,
in increments

of dank brow-panicle

envoi

bobbin-sepulture
leach from pericope
impact canopy

feather-haw brac-
keted with the river's
slough or   slip

fugitive avenue

cowled recension
moving forward (from
what blind copy)

pluvial scotoma

what does "see" see

fringe of analect

fugal hive-carriage

texture socket
-*cum*- planisphere

viscous, stunned
&
hemless, belaying

glyph-hyphen

in abeyance

the ingressing "I"

assessor or
unfathering, *lush*

tonal, the visible
suppuration

oak/synod/suture

or: recall
—*the listening field*

river of
burning glass
(say)
a bridge music

w(h)ither-whisper

vesper's flecked
illumination, cousin-
sphere or -moat

creature errand
shepherd's
conclave / vantage

occupied cross or
fragrant swath

blue smell of
day-glade, nightly

bedding compass

(its musky flute)

thus: estrangement
(the night closes, we say, not
a door but
like a museum, infinite)

bulleted hedgerow
deflects the dusk's motion

take it back, the orphaned
vestas paraphrase

is not like music, camphor,
—"as I conceive it"

(less wounded
though inexpertly Brailled)

the body's hairline
gantry   instills

cadenza   stomata

wheat-leaves
clairvoyant;   bound
in shadow-selvage

concave in cusp-light

back-derivation
of "horse—
to have run wildly
away [from]"

(hymns imagine)

penetralia's
soft-shoe   lotioning

the roadblind
shoulder
(: —move *through*)

eye-clung the wrist
twists into its white dive

I the tattooing
minor key, sepal-bread
or schwa-smolder

the eye withdraws
its stone coracle from

trysting-place:

hierarchy in
emergence, crystal
periphery
exchanging for
knife-pollen
without benefit
of love's
refuse-(w)edge or
spiny plummet

for the singer:
merciless thrum
porrects   &

O valvèd viaduct

mitochondrial
brand or hasp

wimpling hydrants'
bell-blazon

(seedling college)

what has been

—annealed

(unnailed)

& not falsely

overskirted

impact transom

in common

subterfugitive

flusk-glare

a theft unhands

what had been

(interstitial)

pine-marrowed

phantom limb

complex menses

understory

.

testify   (sum or
—testify

aestival boon-harrier
kingdom vein   occludes

a ribbed vacancy
inside the wound-platen's
untarnishing basin

I imagine   distal planes
updrifting, acute angles
made legible
                in cleft-chantry

eleemosynary

thus gender, or gender's
vivid emblem

more (underhanging) sky

G.C. Waldrep is the author of four collections of poetry, most recently *Your Father on the Train of Ghosts* (BOA Editions, 2011), a collaboration with John Gallaher. He co-edited *Homage to Paul Celan* (Marick, 2011) with Ilya Kaminsky and *The Arcadia Project: North American Postmodern Pastoral* (Ahsahta, 2012) with Joshua Corey. He has been the recipient of a National Endowment for the Arts Fellowship in Literature and a Gertrude Stein Award for Innovative American Poetry. He lives in Lewisburg, Pa., where he teaches at Bucknell University, edits the journal *West Branch*, and serves as Editor-at-Large for *The Kenyon Review*.